South Watsonville 1940

Growing Up on Grove Street, 1931-46

Growing Up on Grove Street, 1931-46

Sketches and Memories of a Chinese-American Boyhood

Duncan Chin

Foreword and Afterword by
Sandy Lydon

Capitola Book Company

Capitola Book Company
1601 41st Avenue, Capitola, CA 95010

© 1995 by Capitola Book Company
All rights reserved. No part of this book may
by reproduced without written permission from
the Publisher. Published 1995
Printed in the United States of America

Library of Congress Cataloging-in-Publication Data

Chin, Duncan, 1931-
     Growing up on Grove Street, 1931-46: sketches and memories of a Chinese-American
boyhood / by Duncan Chin; with foreward and historical afterword by Sandy Lydon.
          p.   cm.
     Includes bibliographical references.
     1. Chin Duncan, 1931- —Childhood and youth. 2. Chin, Duncan, 1931- —Note-
books, sketchbooks, etc. 3. Chinese Americans-California—Watsonville—Biography. 4.
Watsonville (Calif.)—Biography.   I. Title.
F869.W28C45 1995
979.4´ 71—dc20   95-30681
ISBN 0-932319-03-3   CIP

For the women in my life —
Verna, Anna, Edwina, and Roberta

CONTENTS

Foreword

I met Duncan Chin at the First Annual Watsonville Chinese Community Picnic in the summer of 1993. He and his family had come up from southern California to join other Chinese community members and their families in reminiscing and reliving the experiences they all shared growing up in the Pajaro Valley before World War II. Several years earlier, I had interviewed some of Duncan's relatives (including his half-sister Alice Leong and several of his cousins in the Chin Goon family) for a book on the history of the Chinese in Watsonville, but somehow I had missed Duncan's family.

Not long after the reunion I received a copy of a group of sketches that Duncan had put together for his family. In a cover letter, the ever-modest Duncan hoped I might enjoy seeing these simple sketches about growing up in Watsonville.

It was love at first sight. As I leafed through them I was immediately transported to the 1930s as seen through the eyes of a little boy. At first it was the little boy's perspective that resonated with me, because I grew up in an agricultural town similar in many ways to Watsonville. The sketches took me back to the apricot orchards of Hollister, the cutting sheds, the smell of sulfur, and the multicultural neighborhood of my youth. While the backdrop of Duncan's boyhood was an apple dryer, mine was a huge tomato cannery that huffed and whistled every fall, sending forth clouds of tomato-laced steam.

Others who saw the sketches also responded with fascination, and the consensus was that the drawings deserved a wider audience. When I contacted my publisher, George Ow, Jr., he was enthusiastic, but we had several projects underway and so Duncan's sketches had to wait. Then, early this spring, the Watsonville Chinese community scheduled their third annual picnic, and George suggested that we put aside our other projects for a moment in order to get Duncan's drawings into print in time for that event.

The ensuing weeks were a whirlwind of telephone calls and scrambling through records to establish names, addresses, and dates and to create the historical background against which to display the drawings. We consulted city directories, fire insurance maps, death records, newspaper accounts, and photographic collections to get the background for Watsonville in the 1930s. We revisited the sites that Duncan had sketched, including Radcliff School (now Watsonville Adult School) and the neighborhood bounded by Walker, First, Main, and the Pajaro River. We found that while some things had changed, others had stayed the same.

Perhaps the most obvious commonality between the 1930s and the 1990s is that Duncan's Grove Street neighborhood continues to be the entry point for the Pajaro Valley's newest working class. While in the 1930s this was made up predominantly of Chinese, Japanese, Filipinos, and Dust Bowl refugees, the folks living there are now Latinos. The auto court on Front Street, which was the home for Okies and Arkies during the 1930s, is now a trailer park filled with Mexican families. The Filipino pool halls, Japanese barbershops, and Chinese cafes along Main Street are now Mexican cantinas.

The faces may be different, but the struggles are the same, a fact that was brought home earlier this year by a flood along the Pajaro River much like the one Duncan lived through in 1938. Maybe that's the most important thing about these drawings. There is a universality that connects all working people in America, and someday when the Mexican immigrants and their children gather in reunion they too will look back with pride on their early struggles.

Many of the sights, sounds, and smells of 1930s Watsonville are gone now, however, and this is what makes Duncan's drawings so important. The only place where the era still exists is in the memories of those who lived there. The neighborhood that is seen in these sketches is an amazing cross-section of cultures — Japanese, Chinese, Slavs, Mexicans, Filipinos, Okies, Arkies, African Americans, and Texies — living and working together. Duncan's world was a self-contained, multicultural ·community of working folks who survived hard times by helping each other.

The word community is used a lot these days, but it often does little more than define a group of people having a common interest. Enter Duncan's world and meet a true community, a kaleidoscope of people from every corner of the world who linked arms and marched, victorious, through a great depression and a world war.

SANDY LYDON

PREFACE

I think John Steinbeck was a little confused in his directions when he wrote the novel *East of Eden*. In my opinion, Eden was located in the Pajaro Valley, a bit north of Steinbeck's Salinas and Monterey. The Pajaro Valley was a paradise of farms, packing sheds, older homes, and a population as varied as its agriculture. I grew up there with Chinese, Japanese, Filipinos, Mexicans, Slavs, Okies, blacks, and off-whites. It was a world of migrant farmworkers and other folks struggling to survive the Great Depression.

The cliché has it that poverty breeds hunger and desperation, but for some folks it sparks their entrepreneurial instincts. The part of Watsonville where I grew up during the 1930s was filled with innovative survivors. Americans, Chinese, Japanese, and Filipinos operated restaurants, cafes, laundries, grocery stores, barbershops, and pool halls. And along with these legitimate businesses, there were establishments that catered to the baser human instincts.

Watsonville's Lower Main Street had more than its share of gambling joints, beer parlors, and whorehouses, businesses that flourished well into the 1940s. Lust and greed lured patrons from far-off cities, and servicemen from Fort Ord and Camp McQuaide came to Watsonville regularly. Of course, there were fights and stabbings, and occasionally a murder or two. Things grew serious enough during World War II that the military officials declared Watsonville off-limits to soldiers. The war and the passage of time brought many changes to Watsonville. The old-timers faded from the scene, and a younger and better-educated generation grew up and went off to greener pastures. I was one of them.

After military service in Korea, I married Anna, the girl of my dreams, whom I had met in Hong Kong during a leave. We settled in Ontario, California, and after being away from Watsonville for more than forty years I am not sure exactly where my roots are now. When I reminisce it is mostly about Watsonville.

Ten years ago I began sketching scenes from my boyhood while sitting in church. It wasn't disinterest in the sermon or boredom that caused me to draw, but a persistent restlessness that has plagued me all of my church-going life. The first sketches were on the back of the church program, but Anna suggested that I get a sketchbook. All of these sketches were drawn in a 5-by-8-inch sketchbook balanced on my knee. When little kids get restless you give them crayons and a coloring book. What do you give an adult? A pencil and piece of paper, I guess.

I am not a trained artist, so if there's anything terribly wrong with these drawings, blame it on my lack of formal training. The same goes for the captions; if they don't interest you, just look at the pictures. In any case, I hope you enjoy this glimpse of what it was like growing up in our own little Eden on Grove Street.

DUNCAN CHIN

Acknowledgments

Much of the information in this book came from interviews with Verna, Duncan, and Shirley Chin during May 1995. Also valuable were interviews with Earl and Evelyn Goon in 1983 and Alice and Henry Leong, also in 1983. Florabelle Wong, a classmate of Duncan's, also helped, as did Lillian McPherson Rouse, a longtime resident of Watsonville. Juliana Cheng translated all the Chinese grave markers in Watsonville's pioneer cemetery in 1988, and her notes were invaluable in reconstructing the Chinese folks buried there. Jo Aribas slogged through the legal records and newspaper files to find wills, death records, and newspaper accounts and also saw this project through the various stages of production. Carolyn Miller edited the text. Chris Lydon formatted and designed the book. And, as always, George Ow, Jr. had the vision to support and encourage the project.

CHAPTER I

—

HOME & FAMILY

Map No. (1)

The place was bigger and more spread out than most residences. There was room to roam and play, along with ample space for gardening and storing junk. It was secluded and isolated, yet conveniently close to town. Our favorite pastime was climbing the highest roof for a bird's-eye view of the world below. The greatest threat to life and limb was not falling, but being caught by Mama. There were also repercussions later when the roof began to leak.

Map No. ②

The crib railing must have been my favorite teething device. It was badly pitted from one end to the other, and white primer paint showed through the green enamel surface. I wonder how I escaped lead poisoning. The little cast-iron stove heated my bathwater and was also used to make coffee and tea, and occasionally to toast bread or marshmallows.

Map No. ③

JIN-GOO
AND CHIN BOY
WITH ANIMAL
CRACKERS

Jin Goo wasn't really this tall, but to a four-year-old he seemed like a giant redwood tree. He was cantankerous with adults but gentle and kindhearted with kids. I looked forward to walks with him, as he never failed to buy me a box of animal crackers.

Map No. (4)

GRANDMA YIN YEE SHEE
PREPARING GARDEN

Grandma Yee Shee was frail but very deter-
mined. She had a great sense of purpose in
life. I'd bet my last nickel she could outlast
any modern-day woman in a day of housecleaning,
cooking, ironing, weeding and digging in the garden.

Map No. (5)

DINNER TABLE -
FRIENDS, RELATIVES
EMPLOYEES ECT,'

D.C.

Communal dining. At least four of the tables in the dining room were occupied by Filipino workers. It didn't seem unusual back then to share meals each day with such a large contingent of people. The experience at the time seemed quite normal, but looking back on it now I can see that it was unique.

Map No. (6)

The first mass-produced Chinese fast food probably got started on Grove Street in Watsonville during apple season, when our resident cook Ah So Suen cooked three hurried meals a day for thirty-five workers and the entire Chin family.

Map No. ⑦

The wooden storage tank behind the house held enough water for a dozen baths before it had to be refilled. Coiled iron pipes beneath the tank were heated by a wood fire and carried hot water to the tank by convection.

Map No. ⑧

Every day was a favorite day at cousin Goon's house next door at 11 Grove. They shared their Sunday comic sections with us, which were our greatest source of entertainment until television came along. The elevated side porch with its two-by-four railing provided many hours of amusement, and helped to perpetuate our reputation as wild monkeys.

Map No. (9)

The back porch of 11 Grove Street on a warm, sunny day. Sheltered and secluded, it was a great place to hang out and do nothing. When it got boring, we swatted flies. There were lots of flies.

Map No. (10)

COAL BURNING
LOCOMOTIVE
CROSSING TRESTLE
INTO WATSONVILLE

The train thundered across the river from Pajaro into Watsonville every day. Sometimes we could feel the train coming before we could hear it. We lived half a block from the tracks. When the train went by it made the ground shake and the windows rattle.

Map No. (11)

Bucky Yue was my very first playmate, and one of the first things I showed him was how to make a flat tire. I remember him as a gentle, sensitive kid who would cry at the sound of a harsh word or unkind look. I was very surprised when I learned that he later became a member of an elite United States Army unit.

Map No. (12)

Tribute to departed ancestors was observed during the Moon Festival and Chinese New Year. Grandma kept tables full of food and drink. The incense disturbed my appetite, though not enough to be noticeable, according to Grandma.

Map No. ⑬

After Papa died, Mama went to work harvesting crops, trimming apples at the dryer,
ironing for cousin See-Goo at his laundry,
and washing dishes at the Star Cafe and Golden
Dragon Restaurant. The last two jobs always gave
her a bad case of dishpan hands.

CHAPTER II

二

THE DRYER

FILIPINO
LABORER
HAND TRUCKING
BOXES OF APPLES

Apples arrived from the orchard in boxes loaded on a flatbed truck, then were hand loaded onto a conveyor belt that took them upstairs. There they were re-stacked and taken by hand truck to the storage area. Later a ramp was built to replace the conveyor belt, and the trucks drove directly to the second story. There they were directly unloaded with the hand truck. We hated to see the conveyor belt go because it served as a fun ride for many years. However, the ramp that replaced it was almost as much fun. We used it for downhill runs on roller skates and bicycles.

Map No. (15)

PEELING &
CORING APPLES

In the old days, all the peeling and coring machines were turned by hand. Workers were paid by the box, so the faster they worked the more money they made. It was very competitive, and jealousy and envy often started arguments and sometimes even fights. Motorized peelers and corers eventually replaced the hand-cranked machines.

Map No. (16)

TRIMMING
DEFECTS &
BLEMISHES

D.C.

The apples moved from coring, peeling, and slicing to a line of women who deftly trimmed worm holes and blemishes with short-bladed knives. It was hard, monotonous work — the machinery thundered and vibrated all day long. Mama put in a full day with me strapped to her back. It was a tremendous effort and an enormous sacrifice on her part. In light of today's work ethic, unions, and restrictive laws, labor organizers would certainly complain that it was exploitation. The women saw it as an opportunity to earn money, and they welcomed the chance to do so.

Map No. (17)

THE OVEN FOR
DRYING SLICED
& CORED APPLES

D.C.

Furnace heat rose from below through slatted floors made of hard oak strips. The smell of sulfur took your breath away, but it eventually dissipated enough to allow the fragrance of drying apples to permeate the atmosphere indoors and out. Ventilation was achieved with motorized airplane-sized propellers mounted horizontally in overhead alcoves. The roar of the furnace and the propellers went on through the night. No one complained. This was in a time before anti-noise-pollution laws and complaining neighbors.

Map No. (18)

B ack in the old days before cardboard boxes
were invented, dehydrated apples were
packed in wooden boxes constructed by
hand with a hammer and nails. In our dryer, the
boxes were made in a gloomy downstairs section of
the warehouse. Albert and Singy spent many hours
down there pounding nails and bending a few as
well.

Map No. (19)

It was long days and short nights for the Filipino workers who lived upstairs above my family. The Filipinos slept on firm mattresses that were laid on wooden platforms. They ate their meals downstairs at tables in the same room but apart from our family.

Map No. 20

The older men sometimes used a device that gurgled and hissed like a living thing. I eventually learned that it was not an opium pipe, but a water pipe, which the men used to cool and filter the tobacco smoke.

CHAPTER III

PUBLIC SCHOOL

Map No. ㉑

Kindergarten was my first exposure to the outside world. I spilled milk on Miss Siefert's dress during milk-and-cookies period. Boy, she was mad. I didn't understand. What was the big deal? After all, I spilled stuff on myself all the time and thought nothing of it.

Map No. (22)

My fifth-grade teacher, Sally Mayer, was the most kind and loving person I ever met. She wrote to me regularly while I was in the Air Force in Korea during the early 1950s. When the letters quit coming I didn't know why, but later I learned she had died of cancer.

Map No. (23)

PA-PA DROPPING
OFF A LOAD OF
STUDENTS FROM
CHINESE SCHOOL
IN FRONT OF
SOO CHOW
RESTURANT

P apa could always be counted on for a ride home from school on rainy days. The Model A panel truck was one of a kind and would no doubt be a priceless antique today.

Map No. (24)

SUMMER
PICNIC AT
RADCLIFFE
LAST DAY OF
SCHOOL

D.C.

The end of school and beginning of summer. What better way to start summer vacation than by having a picnic? The happiness and excitement on that day was exquisite. When we were little kids, a visit to the park for ice cream and soda pop was a big deal. Today those things would be like going to Disneyland or Knotts Berry Farm.

Map No. (25)

Mrs. Rau's persistence helped to sustain attendance at Sunday school. We eventually developed the habit of going to church every Sunday. Both church and Sunday school were held upstairs Watsonville's dimly lit courtroom.

CHAPTER IV

CHINESE SCHOOL

Map No.

CHINESE SCHOOL IN
PAJARO ACROSS THE
BRIDGE FROM
WATSONVILLE

D.C.

C hinese school was our parents' idea. I think most of the kids found American public school tough enough without the added burden of learning to read and write in a language that was, in reality, foreign to them. The school was across the river in Pajaro among beer joints and pool halls in a predominantly Mexican neighborhood. The beer joints played loud music and produced a steady supply of drunks to roam the streets.

Map No. (27)

CLASSROOM
CHINESE SCHOOL

Mr. Hom was a strict disciplinarian, which was probably typical for Chinese teachers in the old days and maybe still true today. We learned to read by rote and practiced brush lettering by the hour. The school budget did not allow for janitorial services, so students kept the floors swept, and each spring we did a complete overhaul of the building with soap and water. I went for 3½ years, and all I can remember now is how to write my name in Chinese.

Map No. (28)

Richard Dong and I incurred the wrath of Mr. Hom on a daily basis. Sometimes he slapped his bamboo switch on his desk to emphasize a point. That seemed to get everyone's attention, except Richard's and mine.

Map No. (29)

Sometimes the shortcut to Chinese school turned out to be the longer way of getting there. Most of the time we crossed the river without difficulty, but occasionally something would happen and we would fall in and get wet. Valuable time was then lost wringing out our wet clothing and building up our courage for a late entry into the classroom. Somehow Mama always knew when we had been to the river. We got whipped for going there and then for lying. Many years later I figured out that damp clothes give off a tell-tale odor.

Map No. (30)

We usually saw hoboes down by the river when we went there. They ate fancy when they could afford steak, but most of the time it was stew or soup. It all smelled good to me.

Map No. (31)

RECESS –
CHINESE SCHOOL

D.C.

Recess was the most enjoyable part of Chinese school. We played on a hard clay surface that turned into a soft sticky muck when it rained. The teacher eventually installed a metal scraper on the side of the back porch steps for us to scrape the mud from the soles of our shoes, but it didn't help much.

Map No. (32)

STUDENT FROM
CHINESE SCHOOL
THROWING ROCK
AT LOY BOCK

D.C.

L oy Bok was an old man who built his home out of corrugated sheet metal. He was unemployed and without income or family. He survived by rummaging through garbage cans and accepting occasional donations. We kids were cruel as heck to him, and though our teacher tried to stop us, he couldn't watch us every minute. Both our teachers and parents tried desperately to correct our youthful ignorance and sadistic tendencies. Loy Bok was 104 years old when he died, and apparently he knew he was going to die because he dug a hole and crawled into it. That's where they found him.

CHAPTER V

五

WORK

Map No. (33)

Shining shoes on Lower Main Street. Many of the men spent their weekend all dressed up and no place to go. The weekend was for rest and relaxation, but there wasn't much to see or do on Lower Main. The choices came down to going to a movie, visiting a beer parlor, having your shoes shined, and visiting a whorehouse.

Map No. (34)

We used firewood for both cooking and heating. Papa cut his share of it as did all the boys in the family. It was not my favorite chore.

Map No. 35

RADCLIFFE SCHOOL
COURTYARD WHERE
CHIN BROS. WORKED
PART-TIME BEFORE/AFTER
SCHOOL.

My brother and I swept floors and cleaned the lavatories at Radcliff Elementary School. The early-morning job was in addition to an earlier morning paper route. George and I got up at 5 A.M. every morning to start the day, and then after school we had janitor chores again. I also washed dishes at the Silver Dollar Cafe until closing time at 9 P.M. George and I managed to go out for sports on top of it all. It was a miracle that we got an education, or passing grades.

NICHOLSON SHED - CUTTING APRICOTS FOR DRYING IN SUN.

Summertime jobs were not plentiful for kids in Watsonville. Every summer, when school let out, Mrs. Wimmer, a grade school teacher, rounded up kids to work at her brother's apricot ranch. Working at Nicholson's Apricot Ranch was an opportunity for students, housewives, and elderly women to earn money by halving apricots for drying in the sun.

NICHOLSON RANCH
RINSING APRICOTS

I t was back-breaking work hoisting five-gallon cans all day long. By today's standards, this method of working apricots would probably not meet the health codes.
The apricot nectar attracted yellow jackets, which were harmless until provoked. I
frequently got stung when I grabbed a box without checking to see if a yellow jacket
was accidentally perched on the handle.

Soldiers on loan from Fort Ord filled a temporary need for heavy-duty workers. The young boys and girls were excited and awed by their presence at the Nicholson Ranch.

Map No. (39)

My buddy from Arkansas (we called him an "Arkie") Ervin Leigh and I sometimes hitched rides to the fields with crews of Mexican laborers. I blended in okay, but Erv's whiteness made him stand out like a turnip in a bucket of tomatoes.

Topping carrots in the Salinas Valley for three
dollars a day plus all the carrots you could
eat. Families could earn pretty good money
when the kids pitched in.

CHAPTER VI

THE NEIGHBORHOOD

Y|ou could hear the sound of the saw from
  blocks away. The firewood cutters were huge
  raw-boned men from the Ozarks. They were
hard working and hard drinking. The saw was driven
right off the truck's rear axle, and the whole thing
screamed and complained its way through large
tree trunks and branches. It spit wood chips and
sawdust everywhere.

Map No. (42)

The Japanese owner of the fishing tackle shop knew where the big ones were and how to catch them. If your luck was bad and you needed a fish to bring home, he could sell you a giant paper koi.

Map No. (43)

There was only one auto repair shop in the neighborhood that I can remember. The Japanese mechanic stayed busy and covered with grease all day long.

Map No. (44)

EIGHT BALL AT
FILIPINO POOL HALL/
BARBERSHOP

The small Filipino barbershop had a ten-table pool hall behind it. When business was slow, they would let us kids play eight ball for free. We got pretty good at it, but not as good as the Filipino pool sharks who hustled soldiers on pass from Fort Ord and Camp McQuaide.

DISPUTE OVER OWNERSHIP OF STRAIGHT RAZOR BETWEEN TONY & ALEX

Map No. (45)

There were two Filipino barbers in the shop, and Tony, on the left, was highstrung and temperamental. His partner Alex was not only easygoing and laidback but also absentminded. When Tony loaned Alex his favorite razor, it caused an ownership dispute that erupted in a fight months later.

Map No. (46)

During quiet times at Tony's barbershop, the customers would take down guitars, mandolins, or ukuleles from the coat rack and give mangled renditions of "Celito Lindo" and other old favorites.

Map No. 47

One of my cousins, Ah-Lok, worked at Jimmy's Liquor Store in the late 1940s. Back then there weren't as many liquor store holdups, but he kept a pistol under the counter anyway. Just in case.

Ah Gnow, the dishwasher and short-order cook at the Silver Dollar Cafe, was amazed at the amount of food that I could eat. One day he bet that I couldn't eat three full plates of food and was willing to put in an extra dollar if I drank a glass of milk on top of it all. Some of the old-timers in the cafe got on his case for endangering my life, but I collected my money. One customer commented that I would probably be sitting in the rest room for a week after all that.

W hen parking was scarce in my neighborhood, Al Cox always had room for one
more car. Everyone took advantage of his
generosity.

"BLACKIE"
INDIAN FRIEND

Blackie was a gentle Cherokee Indian who hung around with the Goon family and worked for them as a general laborer and roustabout. He was strong as heck. I could always count on him for anything. He bought cigarettes for me when clerks wouldn't sell them to me because I was too young.

C upcake Woo. I don't know how he got that name because I don't ever recall seeing him eat a cupcake. Perhaps it was the shape of his head. He always wore a vest with gold chain hanging from his watch fob. He and Blackie were good friends, though Cupcake always referred to him as that "Goddamn Indian."

CHAPTER VII

ADVENTURES

RIDING DOUBLE
ON BALLOON TIRES

The bicycle expanded our world and took us on great adventures beyond Watsonville. Somebody always rode on the handlebars. We went to Palm Beach, a five-mile ride west of town, Pinto Lake, Elkhorn Slough, and every corner of Watsonville imaginable.

Map No. (53)

Palm Beach was great fun. Our times there were lighthearted and magical. When we visited with other kids from the Chinese school, we always had picnic baskets, potato salad, ice cream, and soda. I had the mistaken notion it was all free, but as time passed I realized that someone's time and effort went into the creation of all that pleasure. Running uphill in the beach sand was the ultimate workout. The reward was a spectacular view of the ocean from the top of the dune.

We went skinny dipping on Saturday nights at the Watsonville YMCA. We always swam nude at the Y, and nobody thought anything of it or seemed to care.

S tolen cherries taste better than store-bought ones. This is a fact. If you doubt me, try it. And notice how the flavor is multiplied by a factor of two or three if you almost get caught by the farmer or his dog.

MARBLE GAME
AT E.A. HALL SCHOOL

The game of marbles was hard on our knuckles and knees. We also got chapped hands from the constant contact with Mother Earth. You could tell who the better marble players were by the size of the bulges in their pockets.

Map No. (57)

Behind our house was a huge gas storage tank that belonged to the gas company. Our daily ritual was to heave the biggest rock we could at the tank and make a loud, resounding clang. We knew that we were annoying the gas company workers because they yelled at us. We would wait a day or two and then do it again because it gave us such sadistic pleasure. If you visit the backyard of 15 Grove Street, you will notice a scarcity of rocks on the property.

The dog pound was on the upper slope of the river bank just beyond the railroad trestle. The dogcatcher killed the dogs by shooting them in the head with his pistol, the gun and dog recoiling at almost the same moment. One day the dogcatcher took my friend Alfred's dog, so we decided to spring the dog that night.

We broke the lock of the dog pound with an iron pry bar. It was dark inside the building and the dogs howled and barked like crazy. We took Alfred's dog and his cellmates with us. This was a mistake, however, because a parade of dogs followed us all the way back to Alfred's house.

CHAPTER VIII

LOWER MAIN & THE WAR

SILVER DOLLAR
RESTURANT/
GAMBLING JOINT
MAIN ST. WATSONVILLE

Lower Main Street was at the south end of town, and on it were Mexican beer joints, Filipino barbershops, pool halls, Chinese restaurants, cafes, and back room gambling establishments. On Saturday nights and Sundays the streets were littered with old lottery tickets and empty whiskey bottles. Drunks roamed the streets, and Filipino farm laborers congregated at various spots to socialize, shoot pool, gamble, or seek other recreation, if you know what I mean.

Map No. (61)

Raymond Lew started out with a restaurant called New Home, then started over again with a smaller restaurant next to Lew's Market on Main Street. It lasted for a short while, then he formed a partnership with Hoy Sook in the Silver Dollar Cafe, which was a hole-in-the-wall eating place with a gambling joint behind. I washed dishes and waited on tables and sometimes grilled hamburgers for him.

Map No. (62)

I would sometimes wander into the gambling rooms and watch the games. Mah-jong can be just as addictive as smoking or drinking. If you did all three you could ruin your health and your bank account.

Map No. (63)

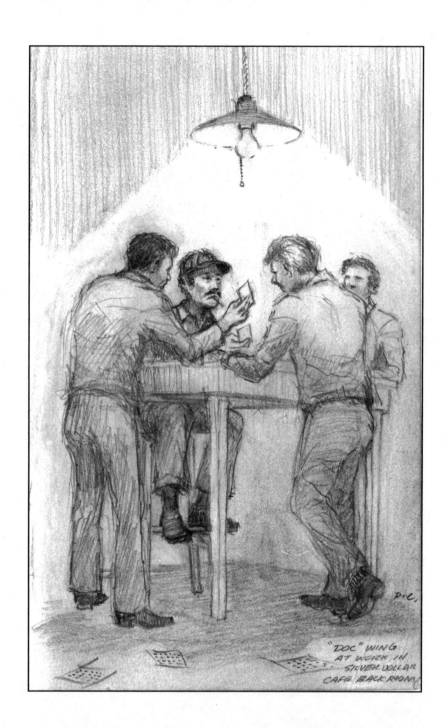

"DOC" WING
AT WORK IN
SILVER DOLLAR
CAFE BACK ROOM

Doc Wing had the look of a gambler. He chain smoked and drank coffee by the gallon. A perpetual smile revealed stained teeth with gold crowns and silver fillings.

Map No. (64)

L ower Main had more than its share of
     winos and bums. Even during the Depres-
     sion, when money and jobs were scarce,
these guys always seemed to manage to scrape
enough together to buy a bottle.

Map No. (65)

The Salvation Army visited Lower Main regularly. You could hear them a block away.
During intermissions the tambourine player would ring a little bell and ask for donations. The brief rest allowed the trombone player to catch his breath before the next performance.

Map No. (66)

MEXICAN KIDS
BEATING UP
NEGRO DERELICT

D.C.

I watched them punch the old black man for several minutes. When I finally couldn't stand it any more, I shouted a challenge at the three guys who were beating him and they accepted. It was a mistake. I was scared, but pride kept me from backing out or running. It would have been a tough fight with just one, but now I had to fight all three. We headed for a nearby alley, and I searched desperately for something to use as a weapon. There was nothing but empty beer cans and wine bottles. Suddenly I remembered what they did in barroom fights in the movies. I picked up a bottle in Hollywood fashion and bashed it against a brick wall. No one wanted to make the first move. After berating each other's ancestry and legitimacy at birth, we went our separate ways. What a relief.

Map No. (67)

When the soldiers started coming to Lower
Main they would approach me with the
question, "Hey kid, where's the action?" I
found out later they were looking for women. I didn't
charge them for the information, though, because
it would have seemed unpatriotic.

The women who hung out at the bars used a lot of makeup and probably needed to. They wore expressions of chronic fatigue and determination to hang on for just one more night. The soldiers from Fort Ord and Camp McQuaide couldn't seem to get enough of their artificial sweetness and whatever else the women had to offer.

RAID AT LING SINGS
WHORE HOUSE.

The women worked in ramshackle buildings
in the back alleys of lower Main Street. Some
of them were not much to look at, but to
lonely Filipino men and desperate soldiers, they
were queens.

R uby Chan was the exotic dancer at the nightclub in the Soo Chow Restaurant. She had a way of moving and positioning her feathers so that you thought you were going to see something. But you never did.

When the war was over, returning Japanese-American students had a difficult time at Watsonville High School. They were constantly being hassled by trouble makers. Their academic achievements, sports ability, and general friendliness eventually earned them the respect they deserved.

Map No.

15 GROVE ST.   D.C.

It's all gone now. Maybe we could have saved it by declaring it a historical land-mark of the American Chinese community. In reality, Grove Street was the focal point of numerous social events for local Chinese and out-of-town visitors. I wish I had tried to save it — somebody should have.

AFTERWORD

by Sandy Lydon

These sketches span a momentous period in the history of Watsonville and the United States. In the thirties and forties, the Great Depression and World War II left their marks on every place and everyone who lived through them. Depressions were nothing new for Watsonville, and the sight of unemployed men wandering the roads and sleeping beneath the bridges that spanned the Pajaro River was not unusual. But the Great Depression of the 1930s brought new faces into the valley, including people from Mexico, Arkansas, Texas, and Oklahoma, who stood beside the Filipinos, Japanese, and Chinese already lined up looking for work. The groups jostled now and then, and sometimes there were sparks. Perhaps the worst moment was in January 1930, when serious rioting between Filipinos and whites broke out in Watsonville and spilled into the surrounding countryside.[1] There were also flashes of anti-Chinese, anti-Japanese, anti-Mexican, and anti-Okie sentiment from time to time. But in general, the period of the 1930s in the Pajaro Valley intensified the things that people had in common rather than their differences, and what they shared was the Great Depression, which had turned their American dream into a nightmare.

In the late 1930s, just when happy days seemed to be around the corner, a cruel world war reached into the valley. The Chinese were the first in the Pajaro Valley to feel the effects of the war. Following Japan's attack on China in 1937, fund raisers from San Francisco came into Watsonville soliciting donations from the Chinese for the defense of their homeland. But the war eventually became democratic, touching everyone. Italian and German aliens were moved off the coastal areas, Japanese and Japanese-Americans were taken away to internment camps, Filipinos joined up to help liberate the Philippines,

Slavs went back to the Balkans to fight the Nazis, and young Americans of every ethnicity went off to war. Those who stayed behind endured blackouts, rationing, and other wartime regulations, and just about everybody went to work to keep the agricultural industry going. As Duncan said in his introduction, the war changed everything, including the city of Watsonville.

Watsonville, California: Apple City

Watsonville has always been a farming town. Located smack in the middle of the fertile alluvial Pajaro Valley, the town developed as a service center for the fields surrounding it. As farmers followed the ever-changing dictates of economics and technology, the kinds of crops passing through the town changed with them. By 1890 the parade included potatoes, cereal grains, hops, and berries. The 1890s saw the ascendancy of the sugar beet, and for ten blessed years (1888-98) the Western Sugar Beet Company hummed steadily at the north end of Walker Street and Watsonville was nicknamed "Sugar City."

An ever-larger labor force was required to cultivate, plant, tend, harvest, and process these diverse crops. Small groups of Indians were sufficient for the grains grown in the 1860s, but eventually it took seasonal surges of hundreds of Chinese and Japanese laborers to provide the necessary labor.

When the sugar factory moved to the Salinas Valley in 1898, Watsonville turned its attention to a burgeoning apple industry, and by 1910 the name Sugar City changed to Apple City. Apple acreage increased steadily during the 1920s, and by the 1930s the Pajaro Valley was one of the leading apple-producing areas in California.[2]

While the apple orchards were owned by people from various backgrounds and cultures, immigrants from the Balkans eventually dominated the packing, storing, and distribution of the apples. Known locally as "Slavonians" (they were primarily Roman Catholic Croatians), these quiet, hardworking people were willing to take the risks of the volatile world of marketing fresh fruit. Like many other immigrant groups, the Slavonians had carved out their own economic niche, using a network of fellow Croatian fruit brokers throughout the United States to distribute their products.

Increasingly stringent standards of quality for fresh apples (brought on mostly by the industry itself) created a large volume of substandard apples, or "culls." At first the culls were turned almost exclusively into cider and vinegar, but the 1880s and 1890s saw a number of experiments in dehydrating culled apples. (Watsonville has too much summertime fog to dry apples in the sun.) By the turn of the century, a number of three-story apple dehydrators, or dryers, dotted the Pajaro Valley, and in some years, the cider, vinegar, and dried apple sales meant the difference between economic success and failure for the Pajaro Valley apple growers. Chinese immigrants and their families eventually dominated the apple-drying business.

The Chinese in the Pajaro Valley

Chinese laborers had been coming into the Monterey Bay Region since the 1860s to fulfill the basic labor needs of the valley.[3] They harvested the wheat and planted, thinned, and topped the sugar beets, dug the potatoes, cleared the willows and tules from swamps and sloughs, and built the railroad lines that connected Watsonville with the outside world. During this period, the sight of crews of Chinese men coming and going was a familiar one as they followed the crops and provided short bursts of labor.

A small Chinatown sprang up in Watsonville, where the seasonal Chinese farm laborers found lodging, food, and recre-

ation. The major recreational activities — gambling, opium, and prostitution — were not G-rated, however, and in 1888 the Chinese business owners were offered an alternative site for their community. After some spirited negotiating, the Chinese eventually moved across the Pajaro River to a more isolated location. The new Chinatown, called Brooklyn after the name of its main street, thrived in the 1890s as hundreds of Chinese came into the valley to work in the burgeoning sugar beet industry.

The Chinese provided more than raw labor in the Monterey Bay Region, however, as they became adept at finding and developing economic niches where they could work for themselves. Because their competition was unwelcome in most industries, they diverted from the economic mainstream, specializing in marginal resources and labor-intensive tasks that enabled them to endure a climate of restrictive legislation, economic discrimination, and outright racism.

But no amount of adaptability could overcome the mother of all restrictive laws - the 1882 Chinese Exclusion Act — which virtually stopped further Chinese immigration to the United States. The cessation of new immigrants, coupled with the fact that the Chinese population was predominantly male, combined to force their population into a steep decline. From its regional high of 2,537 in 1890, the Chinese population dropped to its lowest number — 835 — in 1910.

Agriculture's insatiable appetite for labor did not wane, however, and a new group of laborers entered the fields to replace the aging Chinese, this time from Japan. Somewhere around 1905, the Chinese riding their statistical down escalator, passed the Japanese on their way up. By 1910 there were 689 Japanese in Santa Cruz County and only 194 Chinese; in 1920 the Japanese outnumbered the Chinese by 1,019 to 215, or roughly five to one.[4]

The China Dryers

Apple dryers were three-story buildings in which apples purchased from fruit brokers were treated with sulfur and dried by direct heat. They became the economic life preserver for the Chinese who remained in the Pajaro Valley after the turn of the century. In some instances the Chinese leased the dryers from non-Chinese owners, while others formed partnerships with non-Chinese capitalists. Some of the dryers, such as the one Duncan Chin's family was involved with, were owned outright by Chinese operators.[5] Once again, the Chinese managed to turn a marginal resource — this time substandard apples — into a valuable product. The element that gave them the edge in the apple dehydrating business was access to relatively large numbers of hardworking seasonal laborers (at first Chinese, and later Filipinos). Eventually the Chinese so dominated the apple-drying business that the dryers became known as "China dryers."

The primary difference between the Chinese community in Watsonville in the 1890s and the 1920s was that though the population was much smaller, there were many more Chinese families in the 1920s. The 1920 manuscript census provides the last good detailed look at the community, showing six Chinese families in the city, each having at its core a China dryer. The family names listed included Chan, Leong, Eng, Wong, Goon, and Kee.[6] It is with the China dryer owned by Charlie Chin Goon that we begin Duncan Chin's story.

The Sketches
Chapter One: Home and Family

The story of the Chin family in Watsonville begins with Chin Goon, a Chinese immigrant who came to America in 1876. Chinese traditionally place their family name first, so when Chin Goon told non-Chinese people his name, they assumed that Goon was his family name and called him Mr. Goon instead of Mr. Chin. Over time Chin

Charlie Chin Goon was the patriarch of the Grove Street Chinese compound until his death in 1938. Born in China, Charlie was Chin Yuey's second cousin.

Goon Family Collection

Goon eventually surrendered to the cultural misunderstanding and, taking the American first name Charlie, became Charlie Chin Goon. Charlie came to Watsonville in 1908, and after working briefly as a cook in the Mansion House Hotel he began managing an apple dryer at No. 65 Walker Street. Charlie is listed in the 1910 census as living at that address with his wife Julia, a son Charles and a daughter Hazel. Somewhere between 1910 and 1920, Charlie Chin Goon built an apple dryer at 111 Grove Street; in the 1920 census he is recorded as living on Grove Street with seven children.[7] Charlie Chin Goon's apple dryer, officially named the Western Fruit Evaporating Company, became the magnet that attracted several other Chin relatives, including Duncan Chin's father, Chin Yuey.

Born in San Francisco in 1886 [8], Chin Yuey [9] was the only child of a successful

Jung Yit-sung (Verna Chin) is seated on the right, beside her mother. The two women on the left are unidentified. Photo was taken before her marriage was arranged with Chin Yuey, c. 1927.

Chin Family Collection

that he wanted to take another wife. After considerable consultation and discussion, a marriage was arranged with a young woman named Jung Yit-sung, from a large family in the Toishan district of Canton.

In 1929, at the age of nineteen, Jung Yit-sung left her family and traveled to America to meet the future husband she had only seen in a photograph. "Were you afraid," I asked her in a recent interview. "No, I was not afraid," she said looking me directly in the eye. "Why should I be afraid? He was a good man. There was nothing to be afraid of." According to Chinese custom, Jung Yit-sung did not change her name when marrying Chin Yuey, though some time later she took the name Verna Chin.

Duncan Chin, the first child of Chin Yuey's second marriage, was born in San Francisco on February 9, 1931. Soon after Duncan's birth the family returned to live at

Chinese merchant. In 1890, while on a family visit to China, Chin Yuey's father died. For the next nine years, Chin Yuey and his mother lived in China, during which time he received a traditional Chinese education. He was, according his family, an accomplished musician, and often played and sang traditional music later in his life. Chin Yuey returned with his mother to San Francisco in 1904. While his mother managed an apartment building on Clay Street, Chin Yuey took a variety of jobs, including working for a time as a house boy in the Leland Stanford family.

Chin Yuey married Lim Shee in 1904 and together they had four children, all born while they were living in San Francisco: Emily, Alice, Edward, and Albert. Lim Shee died in 1924, and several years later, Chin Yuey went into partnership with his second cousin, Charley Chin Goon in the Grove Street apple dryer and moved his family (four children and his mother) to Watsonville.

As was the custom of the time, Chin Yuey sent word back to his family in China

Jung Yit-sung, c. 1929. This is the photo which her family sent to Chin Yuey.

Chin Family Collection

No. 15 Grove Street, next door to Charlie Chin Goon's family.

Chin Yuey's older four children and his mother lived in the lower level of the two-story house at 15 Grove Street, while he, Verna, and his growing second family lived in the single-story house at the back of the property. The sleeping arrangements were separate, but the two families of Chin Yuey, together with Charley Chin Goon's family, ate together in a large downstairs dining room in the center of the two-story house. The ringing of a dinner bell (still in the family's possession) summoned everyone to meals from throughout the Grove Street buildings. All the meals were prepared by a family cook, who worked and lived in a small room at the back of the two-story house.

The Chin family compound at 11 and 15 Grove Street resembled that of a tradi-

Chin Yuey and two families, 1932. This formal portrait taken in San Francisco shows Chin Yuey's two sons from his first marriage, Albert on the extreme left and Edward on the extreme right. Verna Chin is standing on the left (and is pregnant with her son, George) while Yee Shee is seated, holding Duncan.

Chin Family Collection

tional Chinese extended family, and for Duncan it was a busy swirl of half-brothers, half-sisters, cousins, uncles, parents, and grandmother. One of the uncles who lived on the premises was the kindly Jin Goo. "Jin Goo loved my children" remembers Verna "He was always holding their hand." Eventually Yuey and Verna Chin added five more children to the family mix: George, Warren, Shirley, Loretta, and Jerry.

Verna Chin remembers her husband with great fondness. "He was a good man," she says. "He never scolded me, and we never fought." Did she ever scold him? "Only one time, when he came home late one night. He said he was sorry and never came home late again." Duncan remembers his father as being a soft-spoken and gentle man. "I spent a lot of time in his lap when I was little," he says.

Following Charley Chin Goon's death in August of 1938, one month before his seventy-fifth birthday, [10] Chin Yuey took over the management of the apple dryer, and in 1939, he purchased it outright. [11] During the years that followed, Duncan remembers his father talking to himself a lot. His new pressures and responsibilities

Chin Yuey, c. 1929. This is the photograph which Chin Yuey sent to China during the process of arranging his second marriage.

Chin Family Collection

might have contributed to a stomach ulcer that eventually required surgery in 1941. "He was always coughing from the sulfur," said Verna. "I think the dryer made him sick."

On April 12, 1942, while Duncan was in town shining shoes, one of his cousins ran up and told him that his father was seriously ill at home. By the time Duncan got home, his father was being wheeled out to a waiting ambulance. Apparently a blood clot from the ulcer surgery had lodged in his heart and, though Duncan remembers his father "fighting very hard," Chin Yuey died at 4 P.M. on Sunday, April 12. "I watched him die right there," remembers Verna. Duncan's memories of that day are dominated by the sounds of his mother's grief: "She cried her heart out."

Verna Chin and her children: Duncan (left), Warren (middle) and George (right), January 1935.

Chin Family Collection

Chin Yuey's family, Grove Street, August 1936. Chin Yuey is holding Warren, while Verna is holding Shirley. Albert is on the far right while Chin Yuey has his hand on Duncan's shoulder and George is in the right foreground.

Chin Family Collection

(Tragedy also struck next door that same week, when Duncan's cousin, Annie Chin Goon, died of tuberculosis at age twenty-nine. She was buried in Pioneer Cemetery just two days after Chin Yuey.)[12]

Verna Chin was now a thirty-two-year-old widow with six children ranging in age from Duncan, the oldest at age eleven, to Jerry, age two. When I asked her about this time in her life, she sat up straight, squared her shoulders, and said, "I went to work. I had to feed my children." And work she did, from picking strawberries ("That was just too hard work," she declares) to working in a laundry, washing dishes, working in the apricot drying sheds, and topping carrots. Duncan remembers the years following his father's death as hard ones. "We all worked," remembers Duncan. "We weren't real poor, but, we didn't have many frills in our lives. Sometimes Julia Goon [Charlie Chin Goon's widow] would bake us an apple pie, or make a crab salad for us. Those were treats we looked forward to."

Chapter Two: The Apple Dryer

The Western Fruit and Evaporating Company dryer at 111 Grove Street looms large in the family's historical landscape. Duncan roamed through it and played there as a child, and Verna put in many hours trimming worm holes and blemishes from peeled apples. Duncan's sketches explain the process: The apples were delivered to the second floor of the dryer, then were peeled, cored, trimmed, and sliced. The trimming stage was dangerous for the women who often cut their fingers, but the most hazardous task was using the horizontal apple slicer. Chin Yuey lost one of his thumbs while trying to clear an apple from the jammed slicing machine.

The sliced apples then passed down another line of women armed with knives, who trimmed out the worm holes and blemishes which had been missed during the first process. Duncan remembers the women who worked in both stages as a collection of Chinese, Japanese, and Mexicans, with a handful of Caucasians. The apples

Duncan Chin (left), his uncle Jin Goo, and the dryer. This is one of the only photographs which shows the dryer. The ovens are on the left out of which are coming the four tall chimneys. The main bulk of the building housed the peeling, cutting, coring, and sorting operation. The heat was drawn from the ovens and out through the top of the building by four large airplane propellers. July 20, 1932.

Chin Family Collection

Looking north on Grove Street, 1938. This photograph was taken from the top of the Chin dryer looking north. The two buildings in the foreground were owned by the Chin family and used as rentals, while the large building in the distance was the four-chimney apple dryer owned by the Valentine family. Grove Street is on the right, and the flood waters from the spring flood of 1938 can be seen in the street. The houses at No. 11 and No. 15 were not damaged by the flood.

Goon Family Collection

were then placed in a sulfur solution (the sulfur helps the apples to keep their light color), after which they were taken into one of the kilns where they were scattered across a large wooden grate through which came the hot air that dried them. The apples were continually turned during the hours it took to remove most of the moisture, then they were allowed to cool. After a final treatment of sulfur fumes, they were packed in wooden boxes for sale and shipment. Duncan remembers his older half-brothers Albert and Singy making the wooden boxes in a gloomy part of the warehouse.

The Western Evaporating Company dryer was known as a "four-chimney dryer" because it had four drying furnaces. Most of the heavy work in the dryers was performed by Filipino laborers, who lived during the apple season in a dormitory on the second floor of the main house at 15 Grove. (In the early 1940s, the Filipinos earned four dollars a day.) The Filipinos took their meals in the large communal dining room downstairs. Duncan remembers the Filipinos going on strike for higher wages after his father took over the dryer in 1938, and for a time they moved out of the dryer dormitory in protest.

During the fall apple season following Chin Yuey's death in 1942, the Chin family rented the dryer to Louis Matiasevich who (together with Pete Matiasevich) then purchased the dryer at an estate auction in 1943 for $8,000. Duncan said that the new owners installed automated corers and peelers to replace the old hand-cranked ones. Eventually the Matiaseviches went into partnership with Louis and Peter Bokariza, but the dryer operated only sporadically in the late 1940s and did not run at all in either the 1948 or 1949 seasons.

In the early morning hours of March 7, 1950, the Western Fruit and Evaporating dryer caught fire and burned to the ground. The heat of the fire was so intense that the Chin family carried some of their belongings over to Julia Goon's porch at No. 11 Grove for safekeeping. The firemen were able to keep the wall of No. 15 Grove Street cool enough so that it did not catch fire, but before the fire was over it had done an estimated $60,000 of damage to the dryer. [13]

Chapter Three: Public School

It was not until he began attending Radcliff Elementary School that Duncan began spending much time away from the Grove Street family compound. The school was

Watsonville Chinese School with parents, teachers and students, c. 1930. This is the building in which Duncan attended classes in the late 1930s.
Florabelle Wong Collection

located about a half mile north on Van Ness Street, and except for rainy weather, Duncan walked to school. His fondest elementary school memories are for his fifth-grade teacher, Sally Mayer. Duncan maintained a regular correspondence with Miss Mayer while he was in the U.S. Air Force, until she died of cancer in the early 1950s. "I was amazed that she never mentioned her illness to me in her letters. She was a wonderful person."

Chapter 4 : Chinese School

One of the main concerns of immigrant parents from China was that their America-born children would not have the benefits of a traditional Chinese education. Thus it became common practice throughout California for local Chinese communities to set up Chinese schools, where the younger generation could learn the Chinese language and something about the history and culture of their parents. Watsonville's first Chinese school was founded in Brooklyn in 1916, but it was destroyed in the fire that also burned most of that Chinatown in 1924. The school was rebuilt within a year at No. 18 Brooklyn Street, and it was this school that Duncan Chin attended between 1939 and 1943.

Chinese school was not just a now-and-then thing for Duncan and his fellow Chinese-American students. Classes began every weekday afternoon about one hour after public school was dismissed and lasted well into the evening. Added to that was a half-day of class on Saturday. Saturdays were set aside for recitation, and each student was required to go in front of the class and recite, in Chinese, what he or she had learned that week. The teachers were from the old school of Chinese education and expected their students to memorize their assignments just as their counterparts in China did.

Duncan remembers going home from public school for a midday snack between

Old Chinese School building, 1974. Located on Brooklyn Street, Pajaro, the distinctive porch and railing were still on the building. The old school building is still there, but the porch has been removed, and it has been remodeled extensively.
Sandy Lydon Collection

three and four, and then walking down and across the river (though his mother told him to always use the bridge) for Chinese school classes from four to about eight each evening. The river bottom was an adventure in itself, and Duncan often passed groups of homeless men who were camped there.

The truth was, however, that Duncan and his friends often took advantage of the teachers. "We were pretty rough on them," says Duncan, "and I think that was one reason they had trouble keeping teachers employed at the school." The other reason, he says, was probably that the Chinese community was not able to pay the teachers well. The school closed in the spring of 1943, and it is doubtful whether the Chin children could have continued attending anyway, given the family's economic straits.

Chapter Five: Work

Duncan Chin can't remember a time when he didn't have some kind of a job. As soon as he was able, he worked in the apple dryer during apple season. Then, as a young boy he shined shoes along Lower Main Street. As an elementary school student, he, his mother, and his younger brothers and sisters worked for the Nicholson family at their apricot drying yard in Aromas, east of Watsonville.

All of the family members worked after 1942, and Verna Chin summarizes that time: "We all worked hard. We had to." During Duncan's high school years he and his brother George had paper routes and janitorial jobs before classes began at Watsonville High School. His after-school jobs included washing dishes at the Golden Dragon and Loma Linda restaurants, and during the summers he did harvesting of many different crops throughout the Pajaro Valley and in the Salinas Valley.

Chapter Six: The Neighborhood

The neighborhood in which Duncan Chin grew up reflected the waves of farm laborers that had come into the Pajaro Valley over the years. Just north and west of Grove Street was a small Japantown that, by 1940, had not only Japanese-owned businesses but also families with Japanese-American kids the same ages as the Chin kids. The Japanese had come into the Pajaro Valley between 1900 and 1924 to replace aging Chinese workers, and this Japantown grew up to serve the needs of the new community. [14] During the decade of the 1930s there were a large number of Japanese families living in and around the Grove Street neighborhood and Duncan had many Japanese-American classmates in public school.

The Japanese moved quickly from being farm laborers to leaseholders and farm owners, and in the 1920s their place

The Grove Street Boys, 1936. Duncan admits that it was difficult for him to sit still, and all the boyhood energy is stopped for a moment in this photograph. From left to right, Edward (Singy) and Albert, Duncan's half brothers; Duncan; and his younger brother George.

Chin Family Collection.

Chin Family, April 1936. From left to right, standing, Albert Chin, Alice Chin, Verna, Chin Yuey and Jin Goo holding Warren Chin. Seated, left to right, George, Yee Shee holding Shirley, and Duncan. Note how uncomfortable Duncan is in the photograph as he found it extremely difficult to sit still. "I look like a coiled spring in this photograph," he said.

Chin Family Collection

in the fields was taken by young Filipino men. Although most of the Filipinos lived in bunkhouses scattered throughout the valley, their recreational and service businesses grew up in and around Duncan's neighborhood. The result was a thriving international business district, including Filipino barbershops and pool halls, Japanese barbershops and related business, Chinese restaurants, bars, liquor stores, laundries, and cigar stores. Added to this mix were Dust Bowl refugees living in the one-room houses between Front Street and the Pajaro River. Duncan also remembers Mexican families living on both sides of the river.

Duncan made close friends with kids from all backgrounds, but he felt a particular affinity toward the kids whose families had fled the Dust Bowl, like his Arkie friend Ervin Leigh, who lived beside the river on Front Street. Other close friends were Richard Dong, who lived on First Street, and Alfred Rader, who lived out on the north side of town. When I asked why he had these particular friends, Duncan said, "None of us were part of the elite crowd at the high school. Maybe we all hung out together because none of us quite fit in."

Did he ever feel the pain of prejudice and discrimination during these years? "Not very often," he said, "but it did happen from time to time, and then it hurt. But I gave it back as good as I got it."

The Japanese, Chinese, and Filipinos living on the Watsonville side of the river had broken the 1888 "understanding" that relegated Asians to living across the river in Brooklyn. The new "understanding" during Duncan's boyhood was that the line was at the Plaza in the center of town. Asians, African Americans, and Mexicans were expected to live south of the Plaza. "Even after World War II," said Duncan, "some of the returning Chinese-American veterans were not welcome up in the nicer neighborhoods at the north end of Watsonville."

The only passport Duncan needed to move freely throughout southern Watsonville, however, was his youth and his curiosity.

Verna Chin smiles framed in the window of the Model A Ford panel truck which her husband drove during the spring and summer when the apple dryer was not running, July 1931.

Chin Family Collection

Chapter Seven: Adventures

The magic carpet that carried Duncan miles beyond his neighborhood was his bicycle. He rarely traveled alone, and there was often a passenger crowded in front of him on the crossbar. Close at hand was the Pajaro River, where Duncan learned to swim. "I'm surprised I didn't die of some terrible disease," Duncan says today, laughing. "Just about everything ran down into the river in those days, and the water must have been pretty polluted."

Duncan remembers swimming at locations ranging from the YMCA swimming pool in Watsonville to Pinto Lake many miles to the north of town, to the south end at Elkhorn Slough and Palm Beach to the west.

Chapter Eight:
Lower Main & the War

Duncan Chin, March 1933. Duncan admits that he has always been restless, and it is no more apparent than in this photograph.

Chin Family Collection

From the very early years of Watsonville's agricultural history, the town had been faced with the dilemma of providing recreation for the hundreds of male farmworkers who came into the valley each year without violating the sensibilities of the rest of the community. The first solution came when Chinatown moved across the river (and into another political jurisdiction) in 1888. It was convenient for Watsonville's city leaders to have gambling, prostitution, and opium close at hand, yet in another county beyond their ability to control it.

When the 1888 "understanding" dissolved after the turn of the century, gambling rooms and whorehouses moved across the river and settled in on the back side of Main and on Union Street. Knowing full well the importance of such activities in the larger economic picture of the Pajaro Valley, Watsonville pretended not to notice.

Lonely soldiers looking for a good time were added to the parade of customers coming into Watsonville during World War II, and as the populations of military camps at Fort Ord, Camp McQuaide (near Sunset Beach), and nearby naval air stations increased, so did the number of servicemen on Lower Main Street. Watsonville gained another nickname during the war: "Sin City." It was not until the 1950s that city officials finally cracked down on the activities and drove them back across the river.[15]

Duncan remembers when the news of the attack on Pearl Harbor arrived at Grove Street on the fateful Sunday afternoon of December 7, 1941. "I remember it was a warm afternoon, and I sat on our back porch listening to my papa and the other men discussing the attack and what it might mean," he says. In the spring of 1942, distracted by the death of his father,

Duncan Chin in Korea, 1952. The Korean War broke out just after Duncan joined the Air Force and he eventually was stationed in Korea as an airplane mechanic. "We kept them flying," he said.
Duncan Chin Collection

Duncan Chin, U.S. Air Force, 1950. This photograph was taken during Duncan's basic training.
Chin Family Collection

he lost touch with his Japanese-American friends, who were taken away to the Salinas Rodeo Grounds and eventually to Poston, Arizona. Some of the homes and businesses owned by the Japanese sat vacant or boarded up during the war. "It was not until the Japanese-American kids came back after the war that I really understood what had happened," said Duncan.

The Japanese received a restrained greeting when they returned to Watsonville after the war. There were quite a few "No Japanese" signs in the businesses along Main Street, and during Duncan's first year in high school (which was also the first year Japanese-American kids returned to Watsonville High) he remembers that they were harassed fairly regularly.

Duncan Chin's Later Life

Duncan graduated from Watsonville High School in 1949. In March 1950, he pursued his life-long interest in airplanes by joining the United States Air Force, where he was trained as an aircraft mechanic. Duncan spent time in East Asia during the Korean War, and it was while on leave in Hong Kong that he met his wife Anna. After his discharge from the Air Force in 1953, he came back to the United States, moving to Southern California to attend the Technical Institute in Burbank on the G.I. Bill. Duncan and Anna were married in Hong Kong in 1956. While attending Glendale Junior College, he went to work for Lockheed Aircraft Service, repairing and modifying airplanes and later worked as a technical illustrator until his retirement in 1992. Duncan and Anna have two grown daughters, Edwina and Roberta, both of whom live in Southern California.

Verna Chin, eighty-four years old at this writing, lives with her daughter Shirley in Watsonville. Verna's other five children are now scattered throughout the United States, but they maintain contact via the telephone and periodic family reunions.

I asked Verna to reflect on what made it possible for her and her family to endure their difficult years. "Patience," she said. "Patience and hard work." But, I countered, did you ever just want to give up? "No. I

The lots at No. 11 and No. 15 Grove Street, 1995. The only thing remaining from the days when Duncan grew up here is a garage (just out of the photo on the left), and the picket fence.

Sandy Lydon Collection

never want to give up. We did it all ourselves. No government help. No welfare." Where did all that strength and determination come from? "It's from being Chinese," she said. "Even when they were poor, the Chinese always worked hard. Always kept going." And then after thinking about it for a moment, she said, "I had six children; the youngest one was only two. I had to feed and raise them. Now they ask me what they can do for me. What would you like to have, Mama? they ask. Isn't that good?"

It is indeed good, and as I drove back through Duncan's neighborhood and past the empty lots where the Grove Street compound once stood, I reflected on the hundreds of working people who were able, despite the worst depression and the greatest war in the history of this country, to nurture and achieve their own version of the American dream. Duncan's family home is gone now; the only building remaining is the garage at No. 11 Grove Street where Charley Chin Goon used to park his car. Also remaining are sections of the picket fence that shows up in so many of the family photographs. That, and the images that Duncan Chin shared with us.

Duncan and Anna Chin, Hong Kong, 1956. Duncan met Anna while on leave in Hong Kong during the Korean War.

Duncan Chin Collection

Notes

1. For a day-by-day account of the riots, see the *Watsonville Evening Pajaronian*, January 19 to January 23, 1930. Also see Howard A. De Witt, "The Watsonville Anti-Filipino Riot of 1930; A Case Study of the Great Depression and Ethnic Conflict in California," *Southern California Quarterly*, vol. LXI, no. 3, Fall 1979. Also see the poem titled "I Remember Fermin: 1930" by Jeff Tagami, in his collection of poems, *October Light* (San Francisco: Kearny Street Workshop Press, 1987), p. 30.

2. Axel Borg, "Apples" in *An Outline History of Agriculture in the Pajaro Valley* (Watsonville: AgriCulture, 1989), pp. 63-65.

3. For a history of the Chinese in Watsonville see Sandy Lydon, *Chinese Gold: The History of the Chinese in the Monterey Bay Region* (Capitola: Capitola Book Company, 1985). Also see Collin H. Dong, M.D., *The Saga of the Dong Family*, reprint of a speech given to the Pajaro Valley Historical Association on July 4, 1971.

4. Bureau of the Census, *1930 U.S. Census Population Abstract for California*, table 17, p. 200.

5. The passage of California's Alien Land Law in 1913 made it illegal for Chinese immigrants to own real property, so if there were no America-born Chinese involved in the business, a partnership with an American citizen was often the only arrangement possible. In the case of the Western Fruit and Evaporating Company dryer, Duncan Chin's father was born in America.

6. Bureau of the Census, *1920 U.S. Census manuscript for California*.

7. County of Santa Cruz Deeds, vol. 272, p. 215. Charlie Chin Goon "in consideration of the love and affection which he has for his spouse" put all the Grove Street property in the name of his America-born wife, Julia. Charlie was probably responding to California's Alien Land Law passed in 1913 which made it illegal for aliens to own property. Chinese could not become naturalized citizens in the United States until 1943.

8. County of Santa Cruz Probate Records, no. 8574. There is a slight discrepancy in Chin Yuey's date of birth. In his own last will and testament he gave his birth date as January 23, 1886, while his headstone in Watsonville's Pioneer Cemetery indicates 1885.

9. The Chinese name order will be used as the family continues to use them. In this case it is the traditional name order, while in others, it will be American-style with family name last.

10. Santa Cruz County Death Records, vol. 1938.

11. Charlie Chin Goon placed all his property in the name of his wife, Julia in 1916 as a result of California's Alien Land Law. Since Charlie was born in China, he could not become a naturalized American citizen, but his America-born wife, Julia was an American citizen. The reverse was true in Chin Yuey's family. He was America-born which allowed him to own property, while Verna was an alien and could not. This is probably the reason that Chin Yuey did not name Verna to receive his real property in his will written in 1941. Chinese could not become naturalized citizens in the United States until 1943.

12. Santa Cruz County Death Records, vol. 1942. In all, four of Charlie Chin Goon's children were struck down by tuberculosis: Charles Chin Goon, Jr; Hazel Chin Goon; Lucy Chin Goon; and Annie.

13. See the *Watsonville Register Pajaronian*, March 7, 1950 for an account of the fire. The last operating China dryer in the Monterey Bay Region is a 1940s two-chimney dryer located near Capitola.

14. See Kazuko Nakane, *Nothing Left in My Hands: An Early Japanese American Community in California's Pajaro Valley* (Seattle: Young Pine Press, 1985. Also see Sandy Lydon, *A Half-Century of Service: The Watsonville Japanese American Citizens League, 1934-1984* (Watsonville: Watsonville Japanese-Americans Citizens League, September 1984).

15. For a further discussion of this part of Watsonville's history, see Betty Lewis, *Watsonville: Memories That Linger* (Fresno: Valley Publishers, 1976), pp. 79-84.

Duncan's world, c. 1923. This rare early photograph was taken looking north into Watsonville. Grove Street is on the left and all three apple dryers on the street are visible. Note also that there are no levees and the towns slopes down into the river bottom. Brooklyn Chinatown in the lower part of the photograph burned in 1924.

Pajaro Valley Historical Association